AF490183

<u>**The Forgivable Sin
by Michelle Bollom**</u>

Table Of Contents

Introduction

I am not a doctor, licensed counselor, psychologist or trauma specialist.

I am simply a woman that allowed the secret and shame of abortion to almost take her out.

I suffered in silence for far too many years. I know what the effects of abortion can do to a person.

I also know the Amazing Transforming and Restorative Power of Jesus Christ and what He has done in my life.

I know what it was like to carry that heavy coat of shame and guilt around and be pissed off at the world for continuing to be so vocal against a decision I chose - and take that disgust from others personally.

I know what it feels like to be rejected unfairly by people, Christians too, for my choice and for now sharing my secret.

I also know what it is like to be free from the guilt, shame and condemnation now.

Many days, I have to pray for those that tend to shout hate. I make a daily decision to cover them in love by taking the offense and hurt I feel directly to Jesus.

 (Not to say some days I don't have my Mr. Bean moments and want to flip the whole world off.)

My hope is to help walk you through some steps to start you on your own journey to wholeness after abortion.

I wrote this poem a few years ago and I want to encourage you if you are feeling hopeless to ***Hold On Pain Ends!***

*The enemy will convince you
there is no hope.
That the restoration process is pointless.
It's taking too long ...
It's too hard...
When will it ever end?
The mundane seems meaningless.
But the mundane is where the
miraculous is birthed.
The day in... the day out...
The baby steps
The big steps
Acts of obedience
Uncomfortable
The small
The big
One next choice
Made moment by moment to
Live. Breathe. Love. Keep Going. Forgive
Surrender to the process
Surrender to His will
Surrender to His timing
Trust not Toil
Rest not Resist
Wait not Wail*

Remain in His presence
Amidst the pain
That is the only place
for the pain to subside
No more
Numb
Confused
Questioning
Why?
Abiding not Answers is where it all lies
Hope is always there...
Hope is the choice we must make
Hope is the method not the means
Hope is relying on His Grace
Hope Is His Saving Grace
HOPE...
Hold
On
Pain
Ends!

~ XXOO Michelle Bollom

Shame Can Only Survive in Silence

*Empathy is the antidote to shame.
The 2 most powerful words when we are
struggling is "Me, too". ~Dr. Brene Brown*

I lived in the shame and silence for almost
25 years before I let the world know my
story.

I had, of course, shared it with trusted
friends over the years that sadly turned out
to be a deal breaker for them.

The relationships fizzled and again my
secret was too much for them to handle.

The rejection of that had me guarding my
secret very tight. I went through years
trying to serve my way in church to pay
penance for my sins. I had seasons where I
wanted no part of God, too.

I came back to the Lord, after my brother and father's sudden deaths, and learning about inner healing work. I then began a deeper relationship with the Lord.

I had shared my secret with a person I thought was a close friend, and sister in Christ; her reaction was shocking. She started to distance herself from me. I was sitting in my bedroom after hanging up the phone from another one of her really vocal and hateful judgements on people that were not Pro-Life, that something shifted for me.

I was trying to share my secret and was being rejected for it.

I remember seeing this prayer….

It stirred my heart to want to stop living in my secret and shame anymore at whatever cost of people's rejection.

Here is that prayer by Elizabeth Crews….

It's time to remove those secret skeletons…

"God who knows our secrets and our longings,
You search us, and you know us.

You know, Gracious Lord, that in each of our
hearts is a locked place;
like a forgotten room or a dark cellar.

We would prefer to forget that it even exists, but
inside it are things that won't stay hidden.

Others would never suspect that we carry such
secrets;
We guard our faces, so no evidence appears, and
we keep our lips sealed, to never reveal the
stories of the skeletons in our closets.

But in the quiet moments, the unguarded times of
solitude,
The doors we struggle to hold shut fly open and
the skeletons, these living, breathing secrets,
come out and dance.
They mock us and remind us of our secret shame.

*O merciful Jesus, free us from the power and the
prison of the skeletons imprisoned in our self-
made dungeons.*

*Teach us that mistakes and brokenness and
failure
are part of creative and bold living.*

*Remind us that what is hidden holds us in
bondage and cannot be healed.*

*Help us to know that nothing is beyond your
forgiveness.
Lead us from our shame to confident joy in you.*

*Let us know the touch of your
compassionate, merciful, and healing love.*

*And teach us to pass this acceptance on to others
who, like us, pretend to be whole while within
them, the skeletons still dance."*

Amen.

Secret Skeletons from Pray with Me, by
Elizabeth Crews

I hope that stirred your heart, too.

Shame drives every toxic thought and destructive behavior we can imagine.

<u>What you don't reveal - can't heal.</u>

Shame can only thrive in secrecy.

The Divine Pardon
The First Steps

*What solace -- what hope! -- we find in the
divine pardon.
It heals us in the most profound ways.
~ David Timms*

Guilt and shame crush our spirits.
Guilt for what we've done; shame for what
we've become. It paralyzes us. And only
grace and forgiveness can renew and
restore us.

I remember thinking, I am Pro-Life now.
I made a bad choice; if I had not made that
choice, I would not have the husband,
children, or even the life I have now.

I began to sob, and something just shifted.
In my pissed off moment crying out to God
*"Why can't people understand I am not
that person anymore…."*

And a ton of other gripes, is when I realized I had never done what I think was one of the first real steps in my healing.

I justified my actions for years: I wouldn't have the life I have now if I wouldn't have made the decision to have an abortion. But it wasn't until I was alone that day that God spoke to my heart and said,
True - you wouldn't have this life but instead of justifying it - try apologizing for it.

Ouch! I am sure I had apologized before, but I suddenly took that as I had never truly repented for making the decision to abort my child.

I had not peeled back the onion enough to really see that I had some deep internal work to do: The first step was to simply apologize for choosing to destroy God's precious gift.

I am not one to sugar coat, so please don't be offended. I had committed murder and here I was just defending and justifying why I did it. I never peeled it back really far enough to say I am truly sorry for participating in the decision of murdering my unborn child.

That revelation and thought alone would have taken me out if I had not come to know Jesus, the relationship, and not the religion, the years before.

 I could have wallowed in my depression over that thought or I could find the hope and healing God was promising if I would confess my sin and repent.

God isn't a respecter of persons - He forgave Moses and David for murder and He said to my heart – *"Don't you think I can forgive you too, Michelle?"*

I remember sobbing so uncontrollably. I actually had gotten face down on my knees on the ground. I simply cried over and over – saying *"How can you forgive me when I can't even forgive myself?"*

It broke something open and off me that day.

The word "repent" means more than mere regret or sorrow. You can be sorry for something and not be repentant. You can feel sorry about a certain sin, especially if you reap the consequences of it.

The person who gets caught in a lie is sorry. The criminal who gets caught is sorry. *But the question is whether that sorrow leads to change?*

Repentance is not a penance for guilt or a quick prayer for forgiveness.

Repentance is a complete brokenness, a change of heart, and a detest of one's own sin.

"A sinner can no more repent and believe without the Holy Spirit's aid than he can create a world. " ~ Charles Spurgeon

Regret keeps you stuck while repenting sets you free …even from our own poor choices and bad decisions.

Restoration always begins with remembering; we have to remember in order to repent and then release so that restoration can begin.

So, let's take the first step and ask the Lord to come into your life if you don't know Him. *Receive your Divine Pardon now.*

Salvation Prayer to Accept Jesus

Jesus, I believe You are the Son of God, that You died on the cross to rescue me from sin and death and to restore me to the Father.

I choose now to turn from my sins, my self-centeredness, and every part of my life that does not please You.

I choose You. I give myself to You.
I receive Your forgiveness and ask You to take Your rightful place in my life as my Savior and Lord.

Come reign in my heart, fill me with Your love and Your Spirit, and help me to become a person who is truly loving—a person like You.

Restore me, Jesus.
Live in me. Love through me.
Thank You, God. In Jesus' name I pray.
Amen.

Once we were asleep, now we are awakened and saved!

Read this amazing poem by Ebigale Wilson

<u>*"The Awakened Bride"*</u>
She has been hurt
You don't have to ask her
Her face tells the story
Of a journey of pain
Of dreams long forgotten
Buried deep under shame
Her eyes reflect
Many stories untold
There was no one to listen
to the cries of her heart
Her body bowed low
crushed by pain and betrayal
No sign of hope to be found in a body so frail
Does she know that He loves her?
Does she know that He cares?
Has anybody told her that?
He is crazy about her?
That He knows her by name?
He's the One who defined her
He's the One she needs most
Her identity is locked up in
What He speaks over her

She will find what she needs
As she moves closer to Him
She will discover her worth
In His deep love for her
She will straighten her crown
She will run on the waves
She will shout to the weary
"Come and take your place!!!"
She has taken His invitation
To passionately pursue Him
She glistens with His glory
She is dressed in His joy
She is stronger than what has
kept her in chains
She has let go of what was
She embraced this new start
She now knows He's coming back
for a spotless bride
So she better get ready
There's no time to waste
She is taking her place
As His warrior daughter
Her pain a vague memory
She is drenched in His love
Undone by His heart
Forever she is overtaken
by the King of her heart.

~ Ebigale Wilson

<u>Your Power Prayers</u>

"Bold prayers honor God, and God honors bold prayers. God isn't offended by your biggest dreams or boldest prayers. He is offended by anything less. If your prayers aren't impossible to you, they are insulting to God." ~ Mark Batterson

Many of these Power Prayers are also the first steps I had to go through to release years of the built-up junk in my soul.

You have asked for Jesus to come into your life and received your *Divine Pardon*; now you are an *Awakened Bride* ready to take your power back.

This chapter is full of *Your Power Prayers*.

Remember: God forgave Moses and David for murder. He has forgiven me and will forgive ANYONE and EVERYONE that comes to Him and asks Him to.

Forgiveness for me, is about obedience
first to the Father, as He instructs us to
forgive as He has forgiven us - that part is
easy. It is the continuous surrender to Him;
each hurt as we journey from that head
knowledge to make it firmly into our heart,
knowing we no longer rehearse the hurts or
offenses, and instead learn to release them
to God.

As we *Forgive Release and Bless* the
offenders.. God heals us.

 (Praying for those that hurt us is a fast
track method to healing our hearts ... not
that they get hit by a bus either - but truly
pray for those that hurt us and bless them.)

This helps us move on without carrying the
toxic wound with us. It's also setting good
boundaries - you don't have to allow them
back into your day to day or stay
connected - you can love them from afar.

Forgiveness Prayer

The LORD is compassionate and gracious, slow to anger, abounding in love. He does not treat us as our sins deserve or repay us according to our iniquities. As far as the east is from the west, so far has He removed our transgressions from us.
—Psalm 103:8-12 NIV

Father God, I ask for Your forgiveness for my choice of abortion. I know Your word above says that You cast our sins as far as the East is from the West, but my sin seems ever so large and looming at times. I repent for not trusting You and making this choice. Help me, Lord, to forgive myself, as well as others, that may have forced this decision upon me.

Prayer to Release Victim Mentality

But in all these things we overwhelmingly conquer through Him who loved us.
—Romans 8:37 NASB

Lord, with Your help, I release all the negative thoughts, feelings and impressions that lead to an attitude of victimhood in my life. I refuse to be a victim any longer. I choose to rely and live on the truth of Your Word that says I am more than a conqueror, rather than a victim, through the One who loves me and gave Himself for me. Let me live a victorious life from this moment on instead of entertaining any thoughts of victimhood.

Prayer to Release Toxic Emotions: Anger, Resentment and Bitterness

Pour out all your worries and stress upon Him and leave them there, for He always tenderly cares for you.
—1 Peter 5:7 TPT

God, hear my cries. You know I am troubled by thoughts and feelings of anger, resentment and bitterness. You also know why. You know how deep the hurt goes and how long I have lived with it. I don't want to live with it any longer. I don't want to be an angry, resentful and bitter person. With Your help, I release all my anger into Your hands. I surrender my resentment. I let go of my bitterness. Help me to keep letting go and release all these toxic emotions as often as they try to return.

"The roots from the tree of bitterness
burrow deeply, when watered from the
spring of unresolved anger."
~Dorothy Valcàrcel

Bitterness doesn't bring healing and it
rarely changes the offender for the better.
Sadly, all bitterness does is eat away at the
inside of the one who chooses to let it live
within themselves. ~Dorothy Valcàrcel

"Bitterness imprisons life;
love releases it.
Bitterness paralyzes life;
love empowers it,
Bitterness sickens life;
love heals it.
Bitterness blinds life;
love anoints its eyes."
—Henry Emerson Fosdick

I want to spend some extra time on the subject of bitterness. It can creep in and we don't even realize it. Here is some information I gathered on releasing bitterness that for a season I had to read daily.

> A wounded spirit who can bear?
> -Proverbs 18:14 KJV

I choose forgiveness over offense.
Bitterness Blinds Me

My freedom does not depend on their resolution – it depends on my resolution.

When I forgive others, I am not letting them off the hook but giving them to God, still wiggling on the hook. I am now off the hook!
~ Henry W. Wright
A More Excellent Way

From the book, "A More Excellent Way" by Henry W. Wright, it continues to give some information on the subject that I found interesting.

Bitterness is a principality; under it and answering to it are seven spirits that reinforce bitterness.

1.   Unforgiveness
2.   Resentment
3.   Retaliation
4.   Anger
5.   Hatred
6.   Violence
7.   Murder

Do a heart check list - remove those spirits and all self-rejection, self-bitterness, self-hatred.

*Look after each other so that none of you
fails to receive the grace of God. Watch
out that no poisonous root of bitterness
grows up to trouble you, corrupting many.*
Hebrews 12:15 (NLT)

Resentment kills a fool.
Job 5:2 (NIV)

*Get rid of all bitterness, rage and anger,
brawling and slander, along with every
form of malice. Be kind and compassionate
to one another, forgiving each other, just
as in Christ God forgave you.*
Ephesians 4:31-32 (NIV)

Dear Heavenly Father, these Scriptures cut to the chase and bring conviction to our hearts. We are Your beloved daughters and sons. It's amazing how quickly a little slight can launch us into a big spite.
Have mercy on us, Lord, and grant us fresh grace, thicker skin and bigger hearts.

Prayer for Repentance

It is because of the Lord's loving kindnesses that we are not consumed, Because His [tender] compassions never fail. They are new every morning; Great and beyond measure is Your faithfulness.
—Lamentations 3:22-23 AMP

Lord, save me from my ways. Save me from my mistakes. Save me from the need to be right or justify my actions. I turn away from it all now, Lord, and ask You to redirect me. I am doing an "about face" now, Lord. I repent, and sincerely apologize for everything that did not bring You glory and was unworthy on my part. I release it now and know that You wash me clean. I thank You for Your mercy and grace. Thank You that Your mercies are new each and every morning.

<u>Prayer to Break Free of Shame and Secrecy</u>

If we acknowledge our sins, then, since He is trustworthy and just, He will forgive them and purify us from all wrongdoing.
—1 John 1:9 CJB

Lord, I acknowledged my sins and shortcomings to You. I need You to purify me and remove the shame that I try to carry. Remove the tendencies I have to want to hold tightly to my secrets. I know Your word clearly tells me in Revelations 12 that I overcome by the words of my testimony. Help me to share my story to help others heal. I no longer have to walk or cower in shame and guilt. O' Lifter of my head, restore unto me beauty from these ashes.

<u>Prayer to Break Trauma</u>

Then we cried out, "Lord, help us! Rescue
us!" And He did!
His light broke through the darkness and
He led us out in freedom
from death's dark shadow and
snapped every one of our chains.
—Psalm 107:13-14 TPT

Lord, rescue me from the torment of
trauma. The endless images that play in my
mind must go in Jesus's name. I bind up
the spirit of trauma that continues to plague
me. I release every fragmented piece of
trauma and cast it off of me and ask You to
restore my soul.
Snap every chain that I continue to cling
to. Remove the darkness and the torment.
Rework and rewire my cells to not hold on
to trauma anymore.

<u>Prayer to Break Word Curses/Vows</u>

Your very words will be used as evidence against you, and your words will declare you either innocent or guilty."
—Matthew 12:37 TPT

Lord, please forgive me for any and all words that I may have spoken that created an unhealthy vow or curse upon my life. I break off every word curse or vow I have made knowingly or unknowingly. Forgive me for speaking ill of myself or of others. For word vows or curses spoken over me, I cancel them and their affects, and forgive those people now. I denounce those words and ask You to fully remove them off my life. In Jesus' Name.

Examples:

"I will never trust anyone again."

Blocks you from trusting others and ultimately trusting God.

"I don't need anyone's help."

Makes you struggle in self-sufficiency and prevents you from asking or giving help without judgements and creates control issues.

"I am so stupid."

Cursing God's Creation

Some vows / curses can include:
I am / You're..
Useless
Stupid
Unworthy
Destined to fail
Horrible person

<u>Prayer to Break Bondage of Rejection</u>

Whoever listens to you listens to Me, also
whoever rejects you rejects Me,
and whoever rejects Me
rejects the One who sent Me.
—Luke 10:16 CJB

Lord, I renounce the spirit of rejection from myself, others, and my ancestors, all the way down my generational bloodlines. I choose to no longer participate in the fear of rejection, or perceived rejection. It has no legal rights to me. I have no need to fear any rejections from others because You never reject me. Change my perception to view any rejection that I may encounter as Your ultimate protection for me. I bind and close the door on all rejection and the spirit of rejection that has operated in my life now and forever.

I want to recommend a book by John Eckhardt, "Destroying The Spirit of Rejection." It is an excellent resource for everyone.

I did not think I needed to read it, but as I started reading it to help someone that was experiencing deep rejection, I found it to be one of the very best resources I have ever found in my inner healing work.

It is available where most books are sold. The book is also full of many prayers as well.

My Saving Grace

Many books inform –
only the Bible Transforms.
~ Unknown

First, let me say that for way too many years, I did not read the Bible.

I had been beat up by it for far too many years in religion.

But when I came back to the Lord, I decided to open it as the Love Letter that it was intended to be for me.

I had a hard time with Proverbs 6:16-20; this verse is what many Pro-Life Radical Advocates (ok, judgmental religious spirited people claiming to be a Christian) will quote making so many people believe God hates us.

These six things doth the Lord hate: yea, seven are an abomination unto him:

[17] A proud look, a lying tongue, <u>and hands that shed innocent blood,</u>

[18] A heart that deviseth wicked imaginations, feet that be swift in running to mischief,

[19] A false witness that speaketh lies, and he that soweth discord among brethren.

[20] My son, keep thy father's commandment, and forsake not the law of thy mother:

[21] Bind them continually upon thine heart and tie them about thy neck.

Sadly, I have been speaking out about this to leaders, churches, communities, and anyone that will listen: Abortion is as much a problem for the churched as the unchurched.

I did Post Abortion Bible Studies in my community through the local pregnancy center. More than half of those attending were daughters of Pastors, Deacons, Elders and Bishops. All were forced to have their abortions due to the shame it would bring their fathers, families and communities.

They all either described how they worked and served hard in the Church trying to prove their good works afterwards or they simply left the church completely because of the hurt they felt because no one offered them anything other than judgement and condemnation.

The World's churches are full of wounded women and men sitting in congregations hurting deeply over this. Another Sanctity of Life sermon and Pro-Life rant will not heal them.

Almost all that I counseled, were still holding onto their secrets and shame so tightly, that many turned to various forms of counterfeit comforts. From hard drugs, alcohol, pills, shopping or food to try to numb their deep pain. I, too, ran to many counterfeit comforts for almost 25 years.

Statistics show that almost 60% of female inmates in our prison systems have had an abortion. Where there is a woman suffering - there are also many men suffering too.

Not every man is the driving force behind the choice to abort. Many men are deeply grieved over their parts or even lack of, in the decision.

My saving grace was learning God's true nature and reading ALL of God's word. God does detest many things, but He also forgives. Completely and fully, He forgives us when we take our wrongdoings to Him. He lovingly convicts us to come up higher. He never condemns us.

<u>The Great Exchange</u>

At the cross Christ made possible a "divine exchange" for everyone who believes in Him. What is this exchange? Because Jesus endured all the evil due to humankind, believers can actually partake in all the good due to Him. ~Derek Prince

God is a gentleman. He never forces himself on you. You must invite Him in.

He is ready and willing to take your pain, but you must first surrender and be willing to give it all to Him.

We all want that great exchange of beauty for ashes - but first we have to be willing to give up our ashes.

In our ministry, Restored Ministries, we do an exercise called, *Release To Live Restored.*

Restored is an acrostic of the words:
Release
Every
Secret Sin Struggle Shame
To
Obtain
Real
Emotional
Deliverance

Some people call me the water lady, because this exercise involves water and some really cool spy paper.

We write down everything we want to release. We exchange the junk for joy. We let go of all that is hindering us and holding us back.

<u>Water is a versatile solving agent.</u>

ver·sa·tile - adjective: able to adapt or be adapted to many different functions or activities. synonyms: adaptable, flexible, all-around, multifaceted, multitalented, resourceful; More

The Lord is the best dissolving agent and solvent I know. <u>Christ; the Living Water;</u> the all-powerful and <u>versatile</u> solving agent that is multifaceted, multitalented, resourceful and MORE
Intervenes
Cleanses and restores us…

He Dissolves…..
Hearts of hate
Minds of lies
Governments of greed
Selfishness of people
Warped perceptions
Division
Racism
Judgement
Evil
Oppression

Sickness
Poverty
Corruption
Laziness
Immortality
Hopelessness
Grief
Doubt
Fear
Trauma
Depression
Addiction
Failure
Lack
Weakness
Curses
Confusion
Despair
Disappointments
Brokenness
Rejection
Rebellion
Worry
And MORE

"Then I will sprinkle pure water on you and make you pure. I will wash away all your filth, the filth from those nasty idols, and I will make you pure. I will also put a new spirit in you to change your way of thinking. I will take out the heart of stone from your body and give you a tender, human heart. I will put my Spirit inside you and change you so that you will obey my laws. You will carefully obey my commands." ~ Ezekiel 36:25-27

I firmly believe there is a purpose in every ounce of pain.
Out of every mess is a message. From every test is a beautifully woven testimony.

Right now, I would like you to do this simple exercise. I will give you a few examples. Start getting comfortable with releasing those ashes and trading them for His Beauty! It's the Greatest Exchange, EVER!

Ashes	**Beauty**
Hate	Love
Shame	Secure
Despair	Hope
Lack	Abundance
Division	Divine Connections
Weakness	Strength
Curses	Blessings
Fear	Courage
Grief	Comfort
Confusion	Clarity
Discouraged	New Resolve
Disappointments	Determination
Sickness	Health
Brokenness	Wholeness
Rejection	Accepted
Rebellion	Obedience
Worry	Peace

Try listing some of your own now.

Ashes _______________________ **Beauty**

If One Is Bound - We Are All Bound

*We're all in this together
if we're in it at all.
~ Johnny Cash*

No one chooses abortion lightly.

Statistics show abortion has lasting affects just like those of PTSD (Post Traumatic Stress Disorder).

Statistics show that those that have chosen abortion suffer with suicidal thoughts, depression, isolation, obsessive compulsive behaviors, addictions, divorce, relationship struggles, and subsequent issues bonding with their future children.

Statistics show that 60% of female inmates in prison have had an abortion. Many will tell you they are in an endless cycle of addiction and crime because of this decision.

We are only as sick as our secrets!

Fear is a powerful driving force: Many are forced into making that decision.
It's never an easy decision.

I took a poll on social media, out of 100's of replies, the majority of people chose abortion because of fear. Other decisions came from being forced by a parent, partner, or family member.

It is forced on many by either fear of the unknown, fear of losing their partners over the unplanned or unwanted pregnancy, or fear of losing the love and acceptance from their disappointed parents and family.

No one ever makes this decision lightly.

No matter what celebrities like Chelsea Handler, Oprah, or Ilyse Hogue, will try to tell you - the effects of abortion are far reaching and lasting for many and not something to be proud of.

But, not something we should feel condemned of anymore, either.

Abortion affects people just like PTSD. It has long ranging effects.

I once even heard of a young college girl that was adamant on choosing abortion. When asked why, she said her Heavenly Father can forgive her, but her earthly father said he would not forgive her if she didn't choose abortion. Her earthly father was a prominent pastor in the community.

Today, as many people around the world are incensed by this topic and decision, we may also be just as enraged and angry for God's daughters and sons that have bought the lies that they are horrible murderers or people, because of their choice to abort.

May we be led to help them receive forgiveness and wholeness instead of simply screaming about how horrible and wrong it is.

We ALL know how horrible it is - trust me. Oprah and Chelsea Handler and every pink hat wearer claiming rights to their choices and bodies will try to spin it differently - but it is never as simple or lighthearted as they claim it is.

May we be able to show them they are loved despite the choices they made and point them to the truth that abortion is not the unforgivable sin. It is The Forgivable Sin!

If you let fear steer your decisions - it only ends up stealing your faith and trust.

<u>Fear is Opposite of Faith.</u>

If "Fear" steers your life you will end up with a boatload of trust issues.
Most people I surveyed said being forced or overwhelming fear: These were the driving forces for almost all decisions to abort.

We have to replace Fear with Faith. We
have to learn to trust again.

Shame doesn't survive when we start to
speak up.

Shame only thrives with silence, secrecy,
and judgement.

Shame dies, becomes annihilated,
with empathy.

I don't want another person to be bound by
the shame, silence, and secrecy of abortion.

If one person is bound – we are all bound.

<u>Please Hear Me</u>

"The art of conversation is the art of hearing as well as of being heard."
~ William Hazlitt

There is wholeness and life and life abundantly available after abortion.

We must shatter the silence and shame by allowing the Words of our testimony and the Blood of the Lamb to enable us to overcome and help others overcome.

I believe the best voices for the future of the unborn lies in the process of letting those that chose abortion know that there is forgiveness, wholeness and restoration available to them in Jesus Christ.

Once they are Restored - they will never want anyone to suffer as they have due to abortion.

I am not here to say abortion is ok or that
we don't have a right to voice our
righteous anger towards the killing of
millions of babies every year.

No, please know and hear my heart-
I am here to say that we must do more - we
can always do more than simply voicing
our anger over abortion.

We can be committed to help RESTORE
lives by helping anyone suffering from the
effects of abortion to become forgiven,
healed and whole. In doing so, we can help
bring about great change to the very fabric
of our Nation.

We begin to repair our stories when we
share our stories.

I want to share some Abortion Stories with
you of how others came to wholeness and
healing after abortion.

Abortion Stories

"You're not a victim for sharing your story. You are a survivor setting the world on fire with your truth. And you never know who needs your light, your warmth and raging courage." ~Alex Elle

Sharing your story is heart work.
It's not easy work, but it might be the most important thing you'll ever do.

By sharing our stories we can somehow repair our stories and help others on the journey of restoration too.

Here are some brave women who took the time and courage to share bits of their stories.

<u>Jennifer's Story</u>

I was raised to be a good girl, but
somehow found myself in a relationship
that I knew wasn't the best for me. From
that relationship I became pregnant. I was
so young and naïve - I couldn't believe that
I was pregnant. Here I was in college, not
knowing what I was going to do. Suddenly,
I was faced with all these decisions and
had such a GREAT FEAR!

I was absolutely mortified to tell my
parents, as I didn't know what they were
going to think or do. I couldn't face my
friends or family. My thoughts were racing
all over the place; I couldn't keep the baby
– I was in college. I didn't have the money
or job to take care of a baby and support it.
Would my parents let me move back home?
Would they support me? What would
everyone think of me?

I kept it a deep dark secret.

I knew that my boyfriend at the time would not make a good father.
I didn't want him to be a part of the baby's life. How was he going to react to the news that I was pregnant?
I discussed the pregnancy with my boyfriend. We both decided and agreed together that it was best for me to have an abortion. In fact, it was really never a question as to what we were going to do. By the time I went to the clinic in college to have a pregnancy test done to confirm the pregnancy, it was almost too late to have an abortion. With no money to pay for the abortion, we pooled our money together as well as borrowed money from his sister.

Going to the abortion clinic was one the most difficult things I've ever done.

As I sat in the clinic, listening to the counselors talk about what we all were going to be facing, sitting and watching all the other women in the clinic, I wanted to get up and run out of there as fast as I could. *What was I doing here??!!*

I knew that having an abortion was wrong, but I faced such a great FEAR in keeping the baby. So many unknowns that I couldn't face. I cried a deep, anguished cry. Again, I kept a deep, dark secret.

For many years, this secret haunted me. I carried so much guilt and shame. Before I married my amazing, wonderful, loving husband, I shared with him what I had done. We both cried, and again, my deep, dark secret was buried in the depths of my heart. It was never mentioned again.

Over the years, I would dream and think of this baby; *how old would it be? Was it a boy or girl? What would it look like now?*

Any talk of abortion, guilt, shame, and fear flooded my mind. I couldn't talk about it and tears would come.
I thought, *"If they only knew what deep, dark secret I was hiding in my heart."* I thought everyone could "see" what awful thing I had done.

I also carried much unforgiveness in my heart – I could not forgive myself for the terrible thing I had done. *If I couldn't forgive myself, then how could God ever forgive me?*

Years later, I went through a terrible health crisis. I prayed and cried out to the Lord. He showed me that my health crisis had a huge emotional component to it. Many emotional layers and heavy baggage to heal from; I knew I could not do on my own.

As I prayed and asked the Lord for guidance to help me heal, He led me to two different ministries, both which were very similar, and both were biblically based.

I never thought I would be a person who would need counseling to help me heal, but God did! All the wars and voices that I heard and constantly swirled around in my mind….Shame, Guilt, Fear, Perfectionist, I'm Not Good Enough, etc. I couldn't handle it anymore and it was affecting who I was as a person but also effecting my health… I couldn't do this on my own anymore.

Then God stepped in – Oh, did He step in! Ever so gently, He healed my heart. To begin my healing, the Lord brought me back to when I was a little girl.

I met Him in our secret place.
One in which I felt safe, secure, and oh, so
loved!

Through the guidance of my counselor,
prayer, and the Lord walking with me and
holding my hand each step of the way,
each layer upon layer of emotional
wounds; fear, guilt, shame, etc. all began to
fade away.

My heart began to heal.

**The scars that were imprinted on my
heart, and the lies that were spoken in
my mind, were all taken away by the
love of Jesus.**

He met me right where I was and loved me
back into His arms. The Lord's grace,
mercy and love was poured into me. And,
most of all His forgiveness! His love for
me never, ever left because of the mistakes
I had made or the lies I believed…I was
His Chosen, His Beloved.

NOTHING COULD EVER SEPARATE
HIS LOVE FOR ME.

For those who are here reading this book,
reading my story and those that have
shared their stories as well, God has
chosen this time, for you, for such a time
as this.

I pray that you feel the width, depth and
love He has for you. The Lord redeems us,
and He turns our ashes into beauty.

Run into His arms and climb into His lap.
Let the Lord wrap His loving arms around
you. He loves you more than you could
ever imagine.

**Nothing could ever separate His love for
you. YOU ARE FORGIVEN!**

Jeremiah 31:3 – "*….Yes, I have loved you
with an everlasting love; Therefore with
lovingkindness I have drawn you.*"

<u>Delinda's Story</u>

Sometimes, we don't understand the weight our guilt carries until the weight is gone, and we are free from it.

Fifteen years ago I had an abortion. My life was such a mess and I had dug a hole so deep; I didn't know how to find my way out. I found myself pregnant in a very unstable situation and at the time thought it was the best option for me and the baby.

I went to a rundown clinic in Nashville. I was disturbed about the things that went on inside this clinic. The environment was relaxed and almost comical. Loud music blaring, and no remorse or compassion for the girls who were waiting to make this life-altering decision.

I saw girls, 13 and 14 years old, with their mom, and watched them get back on their phone as if nothing happened after the procedure.

It was quick and a little painful, but mostly a fog in my memory. I remember letting out one crying gasp afterwards and that was it.

I left, and as I walked out the door, I must've left my heart behind as well.

I chose to pretend it didn't happen because if it didn't happen, I could live with myself. Because of this, I went further in my addiction and became more detached from life and who I was.

My ability to love had also dissipated, and honestly, I didn't think I would ever know how to love again.

When I gave my life to God again, and became faithful to Him, I realized down deep God had forgiven me. I knew this much! But I didn't know how to deal with it or to let go of the guilt.

About three months ago something happened: I experienced an encounter that forced me to acknowledge this child was a "person" and that instead of having two children, I actually have three.
My third child is in heaven.

You see, that's also a reality, I needed to accept. I had believed the lie for so long that I was going to hell and I had never acknowledged the baby was in Heaven, because of this mistake.

Through my spiritual experience, I had to accept my child was a person. "He" was in Heaven and he already forgave me.
Oh' for a moment the pain seemed so deep.

However, as I acknowledged this precious gift as life; the guilt, shame, condemnation, and sadness all began to fade away.

I encourage you to pray and ask God if your child is a boy or a girl.

Ask Him to show you what he or she looks like. Ask Him to give you their name.
Yes, it seemed silly at first and I even wondered, *"God, do you name them or do we?"* But God reminded me of His word: *"Before I formed you in the mother's womb....I knew you....."* Yes, that even means their name.

Once I did these things I could accept my son, Timothy, was a person. He is a part of me, and he is in Heaven.

Your children are in Heaven waiting for you and cheering you on.

There is no resentment or bitterness in Heaven, therefore, your children are not mad or bitter or angry at you. No, they are waiting on you.

God's Word also says that, "He will restore *Everything* the locusts have eaten...." So, that even means your children in Heaven.

There is freedom from any situation or mistake you've experienced or encountered. Even Abortion.

Give it to Him and allow Him to show you how to begin to heal. It took me 15 years only because I didn't acknowledge it.

I didn't know the weight it carried until the weight was gone.

Grab your healing! It's here, it's your portion and it is God's desire!

April's Story

I was 16 when I found out I was pregnant. I was so scared. The father was gone as soon as he found out. I was too afraid to tell my Mom. I went to a lady I babysat for and borrowed the money I needed to get an abortion. I told my older sister, only for the fact, I needed a ride to the clinic.
She was super angry with me, but she took me.

I ended up doing what I thought I had to do out of sheer terror of what people would say or think because of my age. Fear of my parents being angry and disappointed. Fear of raising a child at 16 all alone.

Sometimes, I am not sure I've ever "healed" fully from my abortion experience. I look back and think about that situation so differently since I've become an adult.

I feel shame, remorse, guilt, and grief.

My sister, the one who took me to the clinic that day, tried for years to have a baby and never could. I feel awful that I could have given her a child. It's something that I have had to live with.

Restoration and Wholeness…
I am 50 years old and my journey continues towards restoration and wholeness. I realized three years ago after talking with Michelle that there aren't really any rules on how you believe in God as long as you do.

Once I realized I didn't have to be religious to be a faithful servant of God, I opened up to Him. It was an awesome feeling to let go of some of the doubts I had about God and forgiveness.

I'm not really an advice giver, but, if I had
to choose one thing to say to someone who
has walked in my shoes, I would say;
*"Just do your best every day to be better
than you were yesterday. Be happy with
yourself, we ALL make mistakes. Keep
God in your heart and carry the peace in
knowing He forgives you."*

Elizabeth's Story

The driving force in having an abortion for me, was being forced and fear. Three months after I turned 18, I gave birth to our oldest son. Three months after that, I found out I was pregnant again. My husband did not want another child. We were not yet following Jesus and still living a lifestyle of partying. My husband gave me an ultimatum.

It was either going to be him or the child. I could only keep one. I loved my husband and was afraid of raising a baby on my own, let alone two babies by the time I would turn 19.

I did not want an abortion. I felt abortion was wrong. I decided to get the abortion so that my husband would stay with me. One week after the abortion, my husband left me anyway. He was only gone for a couple weeks and we got back together. Needless to say, I was devastated.

My healing was slow. My husband and I decided to attend a local church. We both gave our hearts to Jesus and that began the first steps to my healing. For a long time, I did not trust my husband. Every time he left for work or to go to the store, I was afraid he was not going to come back. I was constantly in fear. I did a Healing Hearts Post Abortive Bible Study and found some real healing in realizing that Jesus forgave me. I found some real healing in forgiving my husband.

The journey to restoration and wholeness really began when I forgave myself.

Like I mentioned above, I didn't think abortion was right. I went against my own convictions to have an abortion.

Every day I lived with hatred toward myself because I was too afraid to stand up for my convictions, for my unborn child.

As I came to realize this, I forgave myself. I confessed what I did and just let love wash me clean. I knew if I can forgive others for what they do, I can forgive myself.

My final encouragement to someone who feels guilt or shame for having an abortion would be to *forgive yourself*.

Jesus forgives you. You are worthy of love and affection and He is right there to give it to you.

Michell's Story

FEAR – most assuredly – FEAR was the driving force in everything that happened before, during and after the decision to abort my baby. I was 20 years old, already divorced, and had a child who was 2 years old. I was barely making ends meet; living on my own, working 2 jobs and I could not think of one reason that I should keep this child. Not one. I had family and plenty of friends and no one was telling me to make a different choice. I didn't know God then, at least if I did, I wasn't listening to Him either. I was scared. In my mind, I was already a failure. I was not a good mom to my current child. I was drinking, partying and sleeping around and she spent more time with a sitter than she did with me.

Having another baby would only make things worse in my mind. I would feel even more guilty than I already did about every single choice I was making.

I was convinced my child was going to grow up scarred and hating me. *Why would I want another child to feel that way about me?* However, what I didn't realize was the guilt and shame of the abortion, would consume me for a lifetime. I wish someone would have told me that part. Just one person could have changed living my life in bondage, guilt, shame and hatred.

Honestly, my healing came in phases. Looking back now, I see how God used all of these experiences to bring me complete healing. But, it took baby steps.

I put that fateful decision so far back into the recesses of my heart and buried it with a ton of concrete. Nothing was ever going to make me dig it back up again.

Then, in 2001, I met Jesus Christ. And, as He started to break down my barriers, I started to feel true freedom. He started working on that block of concrete.

The first time I confronted the truth about my abortion was in 2004. Here I was on my 3rd marriage (and it was failing - soon to be divorced in 2006) and I was sitting in a service at Lakewood Church. Dodie Osteen was speaking on healing. She initially started to talk about physical healing (that's her true ministry) but for some reason she started to talk about healing from abortion. And dare I say, she was looking straight at me. She spoke about healing, grace, peace and forgiveness. All of this found in Jesus. Yes, even, abortion can be forgiven. And to top it all off, she read the scripture in 2 Samuel 12:22-23 where David lost his baby.

David said, *"While the baby was still alive, I fasted, and I cried. I thought, 'Who knows? Maybe the Lord will feel sorry for me and let the baby live.' But now that the baby is dead, why should I fast? I can't bring him back to life. Someday I will go to him, but he cannot come back to me."*

She went on to explain that the beautiful part of grace is that one day I will see my child again. His forgiveness is complete. Before, during and after, with the promise of something so much more.

I was overcome; I felt the overwhelming love of Jesus wrap His arms around me that day. That was the first day that my healing started to blossom.

During the years, God spoke softly to my heart about it off and on. When I would bring it up, He would bring up Jesus. And I slowly started to believe Him. That I could be completely healed one day. That I could be used for His glory – even in this situation – He would not waste it. He would use me to heal others pain. One day.

In 2010, I met my best friend Heather Renee. She loved Jesus more than any other person I ever knew. She sacrificed it all for Him because of all that He did for her.

Without getting into too much of her story, we had something in common. We both experienced abortions. She was a street girl; a prostitute, drug addict and because of her life on the street, she had 3 abortions before she was 18. At the age of 20, Jesus got ahold of this girl and she was a die-hard servant. When we spoke about our pain in that season of our life, she always spoke about it with a smile. She knew and understood Jesus' promise about seeing her kids one day. And since she couldn't have any children now (because of those abortions) she was holding fast to the promise.

One day, she told me that I hadn't completely healed of the pain and she could see it in my eyes every time we spoke. So, in true fashion, she orchestrated something that changed the course of my life forever. In the span of 2 years, she planned an event where I would speak about my past to a group of women at a conference.

Had she told me; I would never have done it. But, I can honestly say I never saw it coming! One day changed my life forever. I spoke to almost 100 women and when it was all said and done, over half of them shared their stories with me. Stories of pain, unforgiveness, self-harm, hatred, and the list goes on.

Not only that, after the conference was over, I was approached by a woman who worked in a pregnancy center in Brenham, TX. She knew about a pregnancy center in Tomball that were looking for volunteers and she thought I might make a good fit. *What?1? Me?!!? What could I possibly have to offer?*

That day started a fire in me that I could not put out. I called and interviewed with them to talk about what the position would involve while working there. It was a volunteer position, but I didn't care. I was in love with them and I knew I would love the women I would meet in the future.

God always has the way to total healing, and this was where I found it. Not only was I able to minister to other women during their pregnancy, I was honored to be a part of a study group about post abortion healing. I was able to help others see in the healing of Jesus Christ and what I had experienced myself. Talk about a gracious and loving God.

I said that my healing came in phases – and it did. In 1988, I had an abortion. In 2001, I met Jesus. In 2004, I received my first dose of forgiveness. In 2010, I met someone who introduced me to the forgiving of myself. In 2012, I healed some more by ministering to others and today in 2020, I am able to write freely about it.

If I could encourage others in any way, I would say, be patient. Healing doesn't happen overnight. Healing takes time. But it can be experienced, if you allow the Great Healer to do it His way.

It's different for every person.

For some, He may rip the band-aid off. For others, He may have to add super-glue to the wound. And, for some women, He may have to rip it open again for it to heal properly. **No matter what way He chooses, He does it with love: Always, with the most profoundly, tenderly, loving touch possible.** I love Him for that.

Jeannie's Story

The spring of 1970, I was fourteen years old, barely old enough to know how my young body worked. Old enough, though, to notice some weird changes. At the advice of a high school friend, who also needed their services, the two of us took a bus ride to Planned Parenthood.

Her test was negative. Mine was positive.

I don't have a clear memory of telling my boyfriend, although the memory of him coming to our home and telling my parents he wanted to talk to them is very clear.

The four of us sat down in our den. He told them I was pregnant, and we had decided on a therapeutic abortion. The shock to my parents and my fear was palpable.

I was fourteen years old; I rationalized then and for many years to come, that the driving force of my abortion was my age and fear.

How could a fourteen-year-old have a baby? What would I do with it? Too many questions and too much fear to deal with any of them.

The weeks of having to wait for an appointment for the abortion felt endless and stressful. Lots of time to change my mind or have my parents change their minds and help me explore other options. I can say that now, but in 1970, teenage pregnancies were shameful and hidden.

Even though many of the memories of that general time are somewhat fuzzy, the day of June 6, 1970 is crystal clear in my mind today, fifty years later. The first sensation I felt in the recovery room was a sense of emptiness in my belly.

In mulling over my past, I know that shame forced me to keep my abortion hidden. My walk with God today is vibrant, precious, and in complete agreement with the writer of the book of Hebrews. I can attest to the truth of "the blood of Jesus has cleansed my conscience from acts that lead to death in order to serve the Living God." Hebrews 9:14

I became a Christian at sixteen and experienced a real transformation in my life. But, until I was introduced to Linda Cochrane's book, "Forgiven and Set Free" in 1997, twenty-seven years of my life were plagued with shame and guilt.

My walk with God was unstable but sincere. In my late thirties, I began volunteering at a Crisis Pregnancy Center in my community. A year or so into volunteering, I also joined Bible Study Fellowship; it was then my foundation began to grow and become strong.

It was through my daily Bible studies where I learned about God; how to apply His word to my everyday life. It was then, I experienced hearing His voice as He explained the truth of His word to me.

During the spring every year, after my abortion, I would fall into a deep sadness and grief. I didn't understand these feelings were from the anniversary of the abortion.

My Heavenly Father had me in the perfect position for Him to minister to me. The magnitude of the depression and grief were stronger than ever that spring of 1997.

One day, I saw a robin's egg that had been plucked out of its nest; a dead baby robin lay on the grass. Right at that moment, I grasped that my abortion had killed a perfect baby. The same way this little robin was perfect, I knew in my heart it was a real baby I had aborted. This was a turning point for me.

God always has a way out for us! One of the volunteers at the CPC had finished her training and was qualified to do Post Abortion Peer Counseling. She wanted to first, do a one on one counseling, and we were a perfect fit.

I dove into "Forgiven and Set Free" with my whole heart, ready to give it my all. I discovered that God was giving me His all. He opened the eyes of my heart and I saw Him as compassionate and forgiving. Loving me so much, I was not afraid to come to Him; asking Him to help me walk through the Bible study, confronting the truth of my actions, and to set me free.

I could confront these truths in front of the Compassionate, All Seeing, All Knowing God, Who is There. He was my Provider of Healing, Who was Never Changing.

In order to receive all He wanted to bless me with, He broke my heart first as He gave me a glimpse into His compassionate heart. Even though I felt I didn't have the strength to face what I had done, I knew the comfort of His Presence.

At a crucial time in the study, I stopped part way through, thinking I couldn't face anymore. One night, the Lord gave me a dream that helped me profoundly to see the way forward. I would like to share it with you. It is intensely personal to me, but it will also give you an understanding of how deeply personal and intimate our God is with us.

There was a strangely shaped pool I found myself in. At first, being in the water was really nice, but then I realized I felt FEAR.

The water was thoroughly filled with starfish. I batted them away with my hand as they felt horrible. I put my feet down because of the dreadful feel.

I had to call out to somebody to please, LIFT ME OUT, please rescue me; there was no getting away from the horror.

Then, I was in a pool somewhere else. Everything was light and cheerful; Those in the pool were flitting around in glee. In fact, they seemed to be dancing with joy. Then, I lay weary and bloody with Charlee (my dog at the time), THE MOST FAITHFUL ONE beside me; weary and bloody as he was, His eyes spoke to me of the comfort He wanted to give me.

I listened and sensed Jesus speaking," *I was there when you could not see me through your tears. I was there though you could not hear Me through the tumult in your ears.*

I was there to wipe away the tears from your eyes, even though you did not know. This is how close, personal, and intimate I am to you. I heard your weeping.

I felt your sighs as you lay there weary and bleeding; I hovered over you. I comforted you only as a very best friend can. For you see, I felt your pain as I hung there upon that cross. It was for your tears that I died. Yes, you have dreamed a dream of horror as you would imagine it. Remember, I know your fears. I knew you would feel the horror of it; to be unable to move away from that which you would loathe to have touch you. To feel trapped on all sides: For the beauty of which was to turn so ugly, so very ugly, filled with debris and filth.

You could barely call to be rescued, to be lifted out. I would say: Yes, yes, child; even at this most traumatic point, not only was I there for you, I was there for the child.

I lifted that child out. I have that child in a mansion I paid for with My life; That child is ever before Me, dancing with joy. There is no pain here, no sorrow, and no tears.

To that child, I have given an eternal body that shall not be destroyed. The horror was brief; the joy is eternal.

So, as you are ever before Me, as you keep Me before you; think on My eternal greatness. Think on My abilities, think on My enduring compassion; the ways in which I move to undertake for you in all of your ways. There is nothing that is beyond Me, nothing too great or too small for Me. My love for you is complete.

Be comforted by the immediate comfort I extended to the child that was within. Be greatly comforted in knowing that in the greatest time of need, I was there to lift her out. I was the One who rescued her, who lifted her out. I was the One who received her."

This dream brought me great joy. Not only did God show me the way through, He also let me know the child was a girl.

More than anything, it was experiencing the compassion of God that brought me to a turning point to receive His forgiveness; to begin walking in the freedom He bought and paid for - For me - For my actions.

It was so important for me to learn how to recognize and listen for the Lord's voice, so I knew when He was speaking. He is here: Always with us, longing for deeper relationships with each one of us. **Don't let shame or guilt keep you from a relationship with Him.**

At the end of the post abortion study there is an opportunity to memorialize your child, by planting a tree, flower, or anything in which to remember how far God has brought us in our quest for freedom.

I didn't know what to do as a memorial and struggled with this aspect.

One night in my sleep, I realized the Lord was speaking to my heart. I rose and these are the words I penned that serve as my memorial.

A New Dawn

I can see you now in the arms of Jesus
For so long I denied your existence
For so long I denied the fact that you were a
perfectly complete little baby
Real, alive.
With a heart that beat like mine
I was myself still a child
When you came into being
No longer feeling like a child after allowing
your life to be so cruelly snuffed out
But I can see you now in the arms of Jesus
You have a special body now
One that is as perfect as the one you had when
I carried you
Then it was complete. Now it is perfect
You play. You run with joyous freedom
You dance with other children
And you laugh and sing
Your voice sings praises to the King

And you listen with such rapture to the stories
of those great men and women of faith. A
faith I denied you the privilege of growing in.
But I can see you now in the arms of Jesus.
He holds me too when I cry out to Him for
comfort
I've cried out to Him a lot lately as I've come
to terms with what I did with you
I can see you now in the arms of Jesus.
You are safe. You are free.
You have been made new, free from the
horror and pain you briefly knew.
I'm not sure who your daddy was but I know
our Heavenly Father is Father to the fatherless
Defender of the defenseless
And I know that you are with Him
I know that one day I shall come to be with
Him and what a day when He takes me by the
hand to enclose mine in yours.
I named you Heather Dawn.
For as the mist rolls over the heather in the
Scottish highlands, so the Lord has watched
between thee and me.
He has watched and He has waited
He has wanted me to know that He was there

He has wanted me to know He felt the pain of
each tear as they fell. He caught them and has
recorded each one.
Each precious healing tear.
How He has longed for this time when I fully
accept His forgiveness, to allow the truth of
His word to touch me in this place in my
heart.
He has waited and He has watched for the
cloud to pass overhead
And He has waited till the break of day until
the sun broke through.
For all those hours, for all my precious Lord
has completely done, I humbly and gratefully
say, Thank you. Thank You for bringing to
rest, safe in Your arms of love.

In His grip of grace,
Jeannie Pallett

AJ's Story

It's been almost twenty-eight years since I did the inconceivable thing: I had an abortion. The truth to my story is very common like most women experience with abortion. I grew up in an unstable home and I also have hearing loss. I got married at nineteen years old. My husband was violently abusive, and I had one child with him. Two years later, I got divorced. At the age of twenty-two, I was mentally unstable and single. I went out looking for new love hoping to medicate my broken heart and loneliness. Then it happened; I got pregnant.

When I reflect back to that moment it still haunts me. *What kind of logical argument did I convince myself to go through with that procedure?*
The answer was simple: I was broken.

The brokenness in my growing years, crippled my mind and self-worth.

I knew mostly evilness, which obliged me to do shameful things. I felt the decision to have an abortion was my only option. Soon after, I regretted that decision. It was the darkest moment of my life and my internal soul felt like I was sentenced to life in a prison of shame and guilt.

Years later, I decided to accept Jesus as my Lord and Savior. In that instance, I was immediately healed. It was a long journey to get to that point, but Jesus healed me. I knew I was free. I was no longer chained in the prison of shame or guilt. Jesus made me clean and righteous. I prayed to God and asked Him to forgive me of my sins. 1 John 1:9 states, *"If we confess our sins, he is faithful and just to forgive us our sins, and to cleanse us from all unrighteousness."*

God's Word in the Bible gave me the tools I needed to start my life in the right direction. I was able to forgive my past and found my peace.

Today, I enjoy living in the healthy, content moments, with my amazing husband, my two full-grown, beautiful daughters, and granddaughters. I still have the ups and downs like everyone else, however, Jesus is always there to guide me. He gave me the Holy Spirit as my helper as He promises in John 14:16, *"And I will ask the Father, and He will give you another Helper, to be with you forever."*

I have a good feeling that when the time comes for me to meet Jesus in Heaven, it be will be glorious! Jesus will introduce me to the child I had aborted. Until then, I will love that child with all my heart into eternity and hold onto His Promises.

2 Corinthians 4:16-18 Therefore we do not lose heart. Though outwardly we are wasting away, yet inwardly we are being renewed day by day. For our light and momentary troubles are achieving for us an eternal glory that far outweighs them all. So we fix our eyes not on what is seen, but on what is unseen. For what is seen is temporary, but what is unseen is eternal.

Janet's Story

In 1993, I was an alcoholic; unsaved, and living with a man I was engaged to. He was a police officer and an alcoholic as well. It was a pretty difficult relationship because we were Godless and living for ourselves. In May of that year, my mother suddenly died of a massive heart attack. I was devastated. See, the place in my heart, I was to later discover, that was meant for God, I had placed my mother instead. When she died, it felt like I had died. My heart was empty.

I would cry every single day of deep sorrow. After about 2 weeks into my grief, my fiancé, turned, looked at me and said, *"Would you just stop crying. People die every day."* Well, that was it for me. I was done with him, even though I did not tell him that. Every once in a while, when we would be drunk, we would be intimate. Even though deep in my heart, I still hated him for how he hurt me.

One day while I was at work, my boss came in, looked at me said, *"Are you pregnant?"* I had no clue. I never really kept track of my period or anything; I was an alcoholic and I didn't think about those things. Sure enough, I took a test and found out, I indeed, was pregnant.

I was devastated. I hated this man I was with and I was empty inside. The place in my heart that was meant for life, instead, I had placed my mother, and now she was dead. I was bawling as I called my sister right away. I said to her, *"I can't have this baby because I can't love. I have no capacity inside of me to love: It's gone, it's empty, there's nothing. I cannot stay with this man because I hate him. If I keep this baby, I will be stuck with him for the rest of my life."*

How disturbing; but that is how an unregenerate mind thinks.

So, the decision that I made, in an agreement with the man I was with, was to have an abortion. It's interesting, I never believed in abortion as being an option. Even in college, I wrote a paper on other ways to prevent pregnancies, so abortion didn't have to even be an option.
Such a crazy twist in my life at that time.

Another disturbing part of the story: The woman that took me to my appointment, was a woman whose views were life is precious; She was Catholic. She, herself, didn't agree with abortion, but, for whatever reason, she felt in her heart she needed to be the one to help me.
I still don't understand to this day.

It's funny, I don't remember lots of details or many things, but I do remember these details: The office, the visit and the procedure. The recovery room with many beds and a lot of women were in there. It was very cold and very procedural.

I remember when I got back home; I didn't feel good, I was in pain and I was disturbed emotionally. My fiancé was out front, laughing, joking and drinking with somebody. He had no concern about me and what happened that day. I was so disturbed by having that abortion that I ended up seeing a psychiatrist for counseling. That really didn't change my life except it gave me a different perspective on my mother and how I had elevated her position. She never requested to be elevated to it, nor was it an accurate place for me to put her.

Over the next six years, I fell deeper into my alcoholism. I broke up with this gentleman and we went our separate ways. I continued to go deeper, deeper, deeper, into darkness.

And then, on April 5th, 1999, my sister helped me get into Alcoholics Anonymous, where I began my sobriety journey.

God, so had his hand on my life, that two weeks into my sobriety, I gave my heart to my Lord and Savior Jesus Christ. *That day, He washed me clean from shame, guilt, and condemnation.*

I walked in such freedom and such accelerated growth in Christ; It was amazing.

I met who was to be my husband in Alcoholics Anonymous. He was a radical, on fire, born again Christian. Four months later, we got married. We tried to have children and we were not successful. We went for fertility testing and found that we were both fertile, yet we were still not able to get pregnant.

Then, I crashed into condemnation, believing, that because I took the life of that child back in 1993, God was not going to let me have another child.

As I confessed that feeling to my small group, (we were studying Bondage Breakers), a group of them surrounded me and prayed over me that I would still receive the fullness of Forgiveness: Jesus died for me on the cross and I would come to the realization that my Father forgets my sins and washes me clean. He considers me as His pure spotless virgin bride, and nothing would hinder me bearing a child.

July 4, 2002, I gave birth to my first-born son, Nathaniel Xavier Whitmore. I am here to tell you that God forgives, loves, and cherishes each one of His children, regardless, of what we have done in the past. His promises are Yes and Amen.

Today, I have such perfect peace in knowing that I have been washed clean. I've been forgiven of all my sins.

The precious life of that child that was taken back in 1993, is still living in eternity with Jesus. We shall be together again.

I know this because one time when I was at church during worship, I had a vision of a young girl in a pretty Sunday dress with long, flowing hair. She was walking down a road in a beautiful, beautiful place, holding hands with Jesus. I only saw their backs. It was so peaceful and so beautiful. It brought such joy to my heart, knowing my child, is safe in the arms of Jesus.

<u>Carolyn's Story</u>

Fear was my driving force.

My abortion took place in 1981. I was 17 years old. I feared my Dad would kill me if he found out I was pregnant. (My Dad was extremely physically abusive to me, my Mother and siblings.)

I wasn't forced, but my boyfriend at the time, encouraged me to get an abortion. His cousin had two abortions and told me how it was no big deal. I chose to believe her lie.

Over 20 years after my abortion, I attended a post-abortion Bible study, "Forgiven and Set Free" at a church near me. It was the best thing I could've done.

The biggest turning point for me was forgiving the doctor that performed the abortion and forgiving myself.

It took me 10 years to do it. I had suffered for numerous years with recurrent physical pain and the sensation that a hand was grabbing my vaginal opening. I was at a Christian Women's conference in California at the time. I prayed and asked the Lord, *Why do I have this pain and the sensation of someone grabbing that part of my body?* He told me that I had unforgiveness towards the doctor that performed the abortion and therefore the enemy had a legal right to torment me (Matthew 18).

I repented for my unforgiveness, forgave the doctor and was freed from that torment immediately.

I deeply regret having an abortion. But, I cannot change the past. The important thing is to repent to God and receive His forgiveness. **Forgive yourself and any person involved with the abortion.**

Let go of the guilt and shame. They are not from God. Repentance, remorse, and Godly sorrow are important. Once, you have done that and have asked God to forgive you, receive His forgiveness and move on.

Do not stay in a place of self-loathing, condemnation, and beating yourself up. That is not God's way.

Take care of yourself and get the healing you need from the trauma that abortion causes to the soul.

Angel's Story

The driving force behind my decision to have an abortion was fear. I struggled with shame as well; it was equal amounts of both. I was afraid of not being able to afford another child with all the expenses that it entails: Fear of raising a child on my own with no help from the father, shame of what my ex-husband, his family, my daughter, my family, and friends would think.

I had gotten married the summer between my junior and senior year of high school. I was in love but was also desperate to escape battling parents.

I became pregnant with my daughter immediately after getting married and quit going to school my senior year. I suddenly found myself single, four years later, and with no high school education.

In the Fall of 1985, I became pregnant at 22 years old. I was recently divorced, quite heartbroken, and was already a single mother of a 4-year-old daughter. The father was not interested in following through with the pregnancy or being there for me physically or financially, whether I kept the baby or not. I was on my own.

It helped that my best friend had already had an abortion, so she knew where to go and what to do. She told me how easy it was. I convinced myself that if I had the abortion early on in the pregnancy, it really wasn't a baby yet, just a bunch of tissue.

I wish there were crisis pregnancy centers around then like they are now. It might have changed the outcome for me and my baby.

I SWORE after that incident, that I would NEVER have an unplanned pregnancy or abortion ever again!

In 1987, I became reacquainted with a great guy that I had "dated" in junior high in our very small town and had gone to church with when we were younger. We started to date again.

One night, I ran into a childhood acquaintance in a club. I'd known him since first grade, and he was now in medical school. His father was the pastor of a Bible Chapel in our small town. After drinking an alcoholic beverage he bought me, I started not to feel well. I was very sleepy, so I went to the parking lot to go sleep in the car. My childhood friend insisted on driving me home despite my numerous protests. I passed out in the car before leaving the club parking lot. You can guess the rest. I had let my guard down - I was terrified my boyfriend would find out and ruin our budding relationship. I also discovered later that the childhood acquaintance was married.

I never told this childhood acquaintance about the pregnancy. I just made the appointment and aborted another baby. I was NEVER the same after that.

One abortion could be forgiven but I felt like two was too much for the Lord to forgive. I was supposed to know better this time!

I had remarried in 1990 to the wonderful man mentioned earlier. Two years after we got married, we decided to start a family. But first, the decision was made for me to quit smoking. I successfully quit but gained 70 pounds and developed high blood pressure. I became depressed when the weight did not come off. I gained additional pounds and battled depression for several years.

During that time, we struggled with infertility issues.

In 2001, we made a last ditch-effort to get pregnant, in which during that time we discovered I had gone through early menopause.

Our hopes of having a baby together were dashed. Even though I KNEW the Lord did not work this way, I could not shake the feeling that this was a punishment for my abortions.

In 2004, our church began an abortion recovery program. I was really excited and joined the program, however, the program stopped being offered shortly thereafter.

I believe my first grandchild being born in October 2014 had EVERYTHING to do with my turning point.

I never gave up searching for a way through that would work for me. I came to the realization that it was going to have to be a spiritual work to break the bondage I was in that felt impossible to overcome.

In 2015, I found another Abortion Recovery Program through a Crisis Pregnancy Center. THIS PROGRAM CHANGED MY LIFE!!

After many years of praying and crying out to the Lord, I knew he had led me to this place at this moment in time! The Bible-based study we used in the Abortion Recovery Program was excellent and very thorough. It covered every base!

It was through this Abortion Recovery Program that I decided that I wanted to live and be free.

The book and guide we used was, "Surrendering the Secret." I finally began to have freedom from the overwhelming guilt, shame, regret, self-punishment, self-hatred, and depression that had plagued me for 27+ years!
It was being washed away and cleansed by the blood of Jesus! I was finally able to start grieving the loss of my two children.

Following recommendations from my Bible study leaders, I began a sexual abuse recovery program the Crisis Pregnancy Center offered. It was a painful process to come to the realization that the 1988 encounter with my childhood acquaintance was not consensual. That was a huge piece of the healing puzzle.

After I got through the Abortion Recovery Program and the Sexual Abuse Program, I began to co-lead and/or lead the Surrendering the Secret classes at the Crisis Pregnancy Center.

I would encourage everyone to explore a Bible-based Abortion Recovery Program with a group of similar women searching for the same.

The heavy chain around my ankle that Satan used to yank every time I'd get a taste of freedom, was broken forever!

My life has been redeemed through the blood of Jesus Christ and his forgiveness! That's why he died on the cross!! What a monumental gift that we should not take for granted!! We ALL have that available to us as Christ followers!

In 2019, I lost 121 pounds and was able to get off all my blood pressure and other medications. This weight loss journey was orchestrated by the Lord from start to finish. **He helped me to finally remove my "cloak of shame" and this leg of my redemption and healing journey is complete.**

Permission To Grieve

"Sometimes the most healing thing to do is remind ourselves over and over and over, other people feel this too."
~ Andrea Gibson

One thing that really burned me up was sitting in church or at events; it would be Sanctity of Life, children's marches or Mother's Day. I would feel shamed and hurt; grieving my child, although, I know I had made the choice to abort. No one never seemed to offer me the idea that I could grieve my child.

I am here to tell you that YOU DO HAVE PERMISSION TO GRIEVE!

I actually want you to grieve, so that you can move past the grieving stage, which could be keeping you bound to toxic behaviors or emotions.

When I led group studies to help women overcome the effects of abortions through the local pregnancy center, we would do a memorial service at the end. We would have candles and stationery available, so people could write a letter to their child.

Some find it healing to give their child a name and light the candle as we played music. I will include a sample Order of Service as a guide on how you can do this.

My hope is that once you do this for yourself, you will gather people in your community to also work through this step and book together. It is emotional; but very healing.

<u>Sample Letter To Child</u>

Dear Asher,
Precious boy, how I long to hold you in my arms. My arms ache for you. I think about you so often and wish so badly I could turn back time. I would do things so differently. I was afraid, honey. So afraid. Please forgive me, son. Forgive me for not giving you the life you deserved. God had a plan for you, Asher, and I took that from you. I can't wait until I get to meet you in heaven one day. Then I will finally know if you have my blue eyes or your daddy's green eyes. And I will see your smile and hear your laugh. I can't wait! I will hold you so close. I think the angels will have to pry my arms from you that day!
I promise to be the mom you needed. I will love your future siblings with the love I wish I would have given you. I will tell them about you, so they don't make the same mistake I did. And I will tell other women who are afraid and confused, just like I was. Your death won't be in vain, Asher, I promise. Every year I will honor you by celebrating you on the day you should have been born. You will never be forgotten – Never! Until I hold you in my arms, I will hold you in my heart.
Love,
Momma

Example taken from the website strongluv.com

This is one of the hardest parts; writing a letter to your child. I am not even going to try to say it isn't.

It is, however, one of the biggest healing steps in our journey to wholeness after abortion.

I can tell you all that my first letter simply said the words; "*Forgive me my precious child.*" Then, as I worked through the emotions and became stronger, I could pen a longer and deeper letter, as the example I have listed shows.

Don't rush it; pause, pray, and ask God for the words. He is faithful and they will come.

I have saved some space for you to try on the next page.

Letter To My Child

Naming Your Child

Many people believe this is a good idea and a huge step in healing. The thought is that it hurts us to keep referring to our child as, "My Aborted Child."

I have to admit when I first read about naming your child, I thought this was weird. I can't even recall which book I read on healing after abortion that mentions this step.

I thought *"Why in the world would I name them and refer to the child by name? That would cause me more pain."*

I decided to follow the instructions and pray about it.

I probably spent several moments and days alone with God asking Him, *"What was my child, (a boy or a girl) and what was their name?"*

I was so shocked that He actually answered me. This was years before I became comfortable in recognizing the voice of God speaking to me, so I was a bit freaked out.

I know He spoke to me it was a girl; I wrote down the name. I was so freaked out that I ran and folded the piece of paper and stuck it inside a book. To this day, I have searched and searched for it, but I haven't found it. I trust God knows when to bring it back to me.

I have to admit, I don't use the child's name in conversations, it is just strange for me still. I do know, that at the moment I prayed and asked God for a name, He revealed it to me. I found a huge sense of peace wash over me. I am confident my child will be waiting on me when I arrive to Heaven and it will be a glorious reunion.

I say all this to say, do what you feel led to do. We are all unique and if this helps you, great. If you want to skip this section, great too. Let the Lord lead you.

<u>Order of Service Sample</u>

<u>Introduction / Welcome</u>

Play song Psalm 23

<u>Song or Scripture Reading</u>

Read Psalm 51

<u>Candle Lighting Ceremony</u>

In Remembrance Light Candle/s

Have candles and long matches laid out for lighting. Have a lit candle to light matches.

<u>Song or Scripture Reading</u>

Song Goodbye For Now

Read Psalm 61

<u>Closing Prayer</u>

When I led Abortion Support Groups, we ended our studies with this Memorial Service as I mentioned before.
I have added it as a sample so you can create your own.

You can do it alone or you can do with a group of people in your community. Choose whatever songs or scriptures you prefer. This is just a sample to get you started. This was a sample adapted from the abortion recovery study book "Repairing Her Story."

<u>Song Suggestions:</u>
He Has Forgiven Me / Demarius Carbough
Goodbye For Now / Kathy Troccoli
Psalm 23 / Kathy Troccoli

<u>Scripture Suggestions:</u>
Psalm 51 The Message Translation
Isaiah 61:1-9 The Message Translation

<u>Conclusion</u>

I believe God has called me to be a voice
for the unborn by helping to restore men
and women that have made the decision to
abort their unborn child. If we can get
these people to rid themselves of the guilt
and shame, to know that God truly forgives
and loves them still; they will become one
of the greatest Pro-Life movements and
voices for future unborn children the world
has ever seen.

Now, as an Ordained Minister and Inner
Healing counselor, I have counseled
numerous women of all ages that have
shared their stories with me.

I know many that are still too terrified to
share their stories because of their churches
and pastors that are so vocal about their
disgust and opinions on abortion.

I encourage Pastors and leaders to please stop alienating your wounded women and men and instead realize - the children are not the only victims. Send those in your congregations that are suffering to Restored Ministries. We would love to help them.

In my studies with post abortion women, more than half of the groups were daughters of Pastors, Bishops, or Elders in the church.

Abortion is just as much a problem for the churched as it is the unchurched.

Harsh judgements and opinions, regarding abortion, is also what keeps many out of the church. It keeps many overly serving in church, as well, trying to earn their way to Heaven.

Both reasons still keep them suffering in silence and fear of releasing this secret.

Abortion is not the unforgivable sin as you would be led to believe. God does not have a grading scale on sins either.

God forgave Moses and David for murder. God can and does forgive you, too!

If you are tired of suffering in silence and need someone to talk to, contact me. I would love to listen, pray with you and help you to finally #LiveRestored - Mind Body & Soul.

Let's #ShatterTheSilence and #ShoutOurJesus together, and finally break the silence, shame and suffering of abortion.

~XXOO Michelle Bollom

RestoredMinistries.org

<u>God's Promises</u>

Therefore, there is now no condemnation
for those who are in Christ Jesus.
~Romans 8:1 NIV

Stop dwelling on the past. Don't even
remember these former things.
I am doing something brand new,
something unheard of.
~Isaiah 43:18-19 TPT

Pain handled in God's way produces a
turning from sin to God which leads to
salvation, and there is nothing to regret in
that! But pain handled in the world's way
produces only death.
~2 Corinthians 7:10 CJB

You did it: You turned my deepest pains
into joyful dancing;
You stripped off my dark clothing
and covered me with joyful light.
~Psalm 30:11 The Voice

Please! Forgive the offense of this people according to the greatness of your grace, just as you have borne with this people from Egypt until now." *Adonai* answered, "I have forgiven, as you have asked.
~Numbers 14:19-20 CJB

"Come now," says *Adonai*, "let's talk this over together. Even if your sins are like scarlet, they will be white as snow; even if they are red as crimson, they will be like wool. ~Isaiah 1:18 CJB

He is so rich in kindness and grace that he purchased our freedom with the blood of his Son and forgave our sins.
~Ephesians 1:7 NLT

I have blotted out your transgressions like a cloud and your sins like a mist.
~Isaiah 44:22 ESV

Get rid of all bitterness, rage and anger,
brawling and slander, along with every
form of malice. Be kind and compassionate
to one another, forgiving each other, just as
in Christ God forgave you.
~Ephesians 4:31-32 NIV

He will wipe all tears from their eyes, and
there will be no more death, suffering,
crying, or pain. These things of the past are
gone forever.
~ Revelation 21:4 CEV

Great is our Lord and abundant in strength;
His understanding is infinite. The Lord
supports the afflicted;
~ Psalm 147:5-6 NASB

The LORD is compassionate and gracious,
slow to anger, abounding in love, He does
not treat us as our sins deserve or repay us
according to our iniquities. as far as the
east is from the west, so far has he
removed our transgressions from us.
~Psalm 103:8-12 NIV

But in all these things we
overwhelmingly conquer through Him who
loved us.
~Romans 8:37 NASB

Pour out all your worries and stress upon
Him and leave them there, for He always
tenderly cares for you.
~1 Peter 5:7 TPT

It is because of the Lord's loving
kindnesses that we are not consumed,
Because His [tender] compassions never
fail. They are new every morning; Great
and beyond measure is Your faithfulness.
~Lamentations 3:22-23 AMP

If we acknowledge our sins, then, since He
is trustworthy and just, He will forgive
them and purify us from all wrongdoing.
~1 John 1:9 CJB

A healthy spirit conquers adversity, but
what can you do when the spirit is
crushed?
~Proverbs 18:14 MSG

Look after each other so that not one of
you will fail to find God's best blessings.
Watch out that no bitterness takes root
among you, for as it springs up it causes
deep trouble, hurting many in their
spiritual lives.
~Hebrews 12:15 TLB

A fool's anger will kill him. His jealousy
will destroy him.
~Job 5:2 ERV

Then we cried out, "Lord, help us! Rescue
us!" And He did! His light broke through
the darkness and He led us out in freedom
from death's dark shadow and snapped
every one of our chains.
~ Psalm 107:13-14 TPT

Your very words will be used as evidence
against you, and your words will declare
you either innocent or guilty.
~Matthew 12:37 TPT

The one who listens to you listens to Me;
and the one who rejects you rejects Me;
and the one who rejects Me rejects Him
[My heavenly Father] who sent Me.
~Luke 10:16 AMP

Then I will sprinkle clean water on you,
and you will be clean; I will cleanse you
from all your uncleanness and from all
your idols. Moreover, I will give you a
new heart and put a new spirit within you,
and I will remove the heart of stone from
your flesh and give you a heart of flesh. I
will put my Spirit within you and cause
you to walk in My statutes, and you will
keep My ordinances and do them. You will
live in the land that I gave to your fathers;
and you will be My people, and I will be
your God.
~Ezekiel 36:25-28 AMP

I have loved you with an everlasting
love— out of faithfulness I have drawn
you close.
~Jeremiah 31:1 VOICE

Generous in love—God, give grace! Huge
in mercy—wipe out my bad record. Scrub
away my guilt, soak out my sins in your
laundry. I know how bad I've been; my
sins are staring me down. You're the One
I've violated, and you've seen it all, seen
the full extent of my evil. You have all the
facts before you; whatever you decide
about me is fair. I've been out of step with
you for a long time, in the wrong since
before I was born. What you're after is
truth from the inside out. Enter me, then;
conceive a new, true life. Soak me in your
laundry and I'll come out clean, scrub me
and I'll have a snow-white life.
Tune me in to foot-tapping songs, set these
once-broken bones to dancing.

Don't look too close for blemishes, give
me a clean bill of health. God, make a
fresh start in me, shape a Genesis week
from the chaos of my life. Don't throw me
out with the trash; or fail to breathe
holiness in me. Bring me back from gray
exile, put a fresh wind in my sails!
Give me a job teaching rebels your ways
so the lost can find their way home.
Commute my death sentence, God, my
salvation God, and I'll sing anthems to
your life-giving ways. Unbutton my lips,
dear God; I'll let loose with your praise.
Going through the motions doesn't please
you, a flawless performance is nothing to
you. I learned God-worship when my pride
was shattered. Heart-shattered lives ready
for love don't for a moment escape God's
notice. Make Zion the place you delight in,
repair Jerusalem's broken-down walls.
Then you'll get real worship from us, acts
of worship small and large, Including all
the bulls they can heave onto your altar!
~Psalm 51 The Message

The Spirit of GOD, the Master, is on me
because God anointed me. He sent me to
preach good news to the poor, heal the
heartbroken, Announce freedom to all
captives, pardon all prisoners. GOD sent
me to announce the year of his grace— a
celebration of God's destruction of our
enemies— and to comfort all who mourn,
To care for the needs of all who mourn in
Zion, give them bouquets of roses instead
of ashes, Messages of joy instead of news
of doom, a praising heart instead of a
languid spirit. Rename them "Oaks of
Righteousness" planted by GOD to display
his glory. They'll rebuild the old ruins,
raise a new city out of the wreckage.
They'll start over on the ruined cities, take
the rubble left behind and make it new.
You'll hire outsiders to herd your flocks
and foreigners to work your fields, But
you'll have the title "Priests of GOD ,"
honored as ministers of our God. You'll
feast on the bounty of nations; you'll bask
in their glory.

Because you got a double dose of trouble
and more than your share of contempt,
Your inheritance in the land will be
doubled and your joy go on forever.
"Because I, GOD, love fair dealing and
hate thievery and crime, I'll pay your
wages on time and in full, and establish my
eternal covenant with you. Your
descendants will become well-known all
over. Your children in foreign countries
Will be recognized at once as the people I
have blessed."
~Isaiah 61:1-9 The Message

Use the next few pages to write your own
Promises of God. I like to write them in
first person and read them each day to
remind myself.

My Promises

My Promises

My Promises

<u>My Promises</u>

<h1 style="text-align:center"><u>Acknowledgements</u></h1>

I want to first and foremost give thanks and praise to My Lord and Savior Jesus Christ, for completely transforming my life.

For my family that walked every step of this journey with me, those here and those that have passed, thank you, for your unending love and support.

This book was six years in the making. At times, it seemed it would never be finished; Then God brought an amazing person across my path.

A Divine Connection from across the miles. A kindred soul and Sister that He knew I needed. Jennifer Wedan, I cannot thank you enough for your friendship, prophetic words, encouragement, prayers, support, and ultimately the care of this book. Your editing skills and attention to details helped me immensely. I love you!

We're Only As Sick As Our Secrets!

For over twenty-five years I kept a secret that almost killed me.

I suffered in shame and silence believing I had committed the unforgivable sin.

What I didn't know is that 1.3 million women a year make the same choice I did, but many are still suffering in shame and silence.

This is my journey.

Come start your healing journey today.

There is hope, healing, and wholeness available for you after abortion.

For more information, books, and resources check out RestoredMinistries.org